JUST SMALL THINGS

COLORING BOOK

by Julianne Colors
www.juliannecolors.com

CATBUTT CREATIONS, LLC

ISBN: 9798842302697

Thank you!

Thank you so much for purchasing my coloring book! I hope you enjoy it as much as I loved creating it!

This book was inspired by the feedback of my followers on social media. If you'd like to follow me and give me your feedback on future books, please find me on social media:

TIKTOK: @juliannecolors

facebook.com/juliannecolors

INSTAGRAM: @juliannecolors

pinterest.com/Juliannecolors

YOUTUBE Channel: Julianne Colors

TEST PAGE

Use this page to test your coloring mediums.

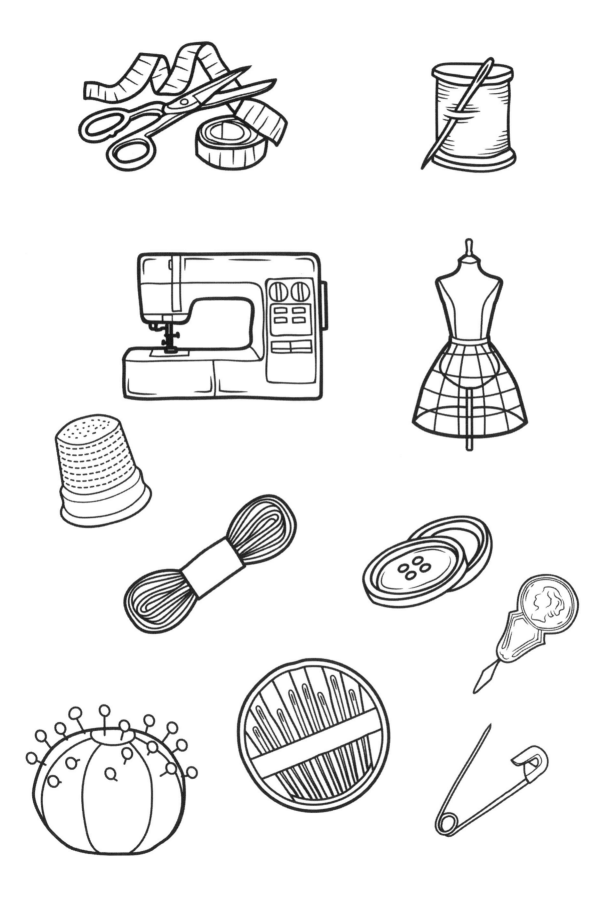

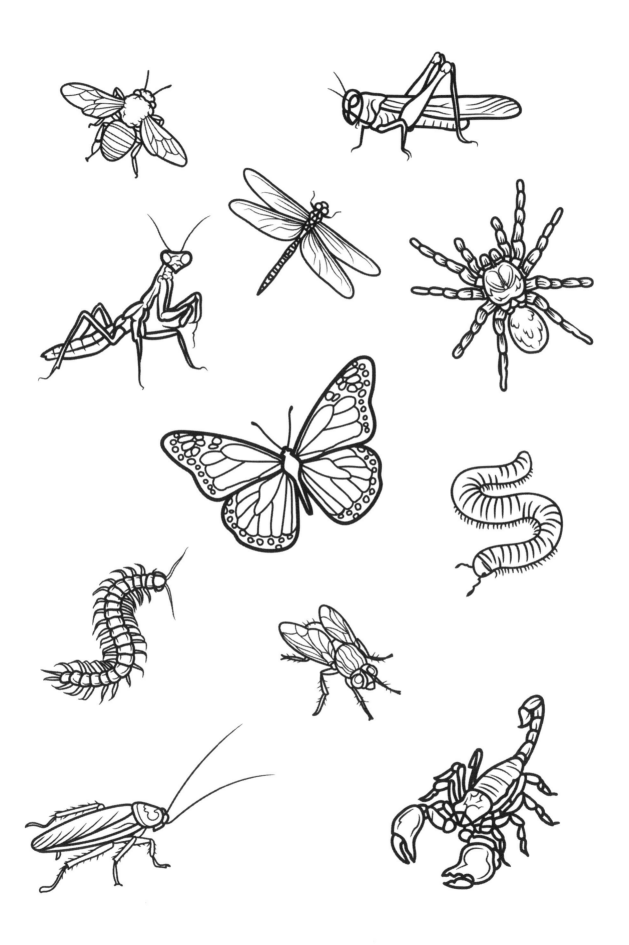

Made in the USA
Las Vegas, NV
29 March 2024

87974201R00050